Living
LIFE
Wise
Increases
SMILE
Size!

Heather Aguilar

Ordering Information:

Prime Seven Media
518 Landmann St.
Tomah City, WI 54660

Printed in the United States of America

#1

CHOICES in LIFE
on the WAY

Take 1

It's important to step back
and LOOK at the scene
To understand Life's Lessons
and what they TRULY mean.
Often times they aren't as painful
as they are perceived to be
For they're usually a prescription
to improve the way we see
How the choice that caused the trip
and catastrophic final fall
Was actually preventable from
happening at all!
To comprehend "TAKE 1" and
see the matter of the fact
Assists in keeping "TAKE 2"
aligned along the track!

~Heather Aguilar
© January 19, 2009

Embrace the Fact, Perform the Act

Individuals on earth apply for the positions
Of managing their leader's
profound divine commissions.

Yet, those hired for the task in the end will only be
The ones who've pre-researched and
the truth in heart can see.

Many without the same view have
completed applications
And mock those who have researched
with inner motivation

The bumpy path along the way
towards actually being hired
is worth it in the end because the title is acquired.

Those who've secured the positions
hold the honor to share
Their wisdom of the answers to
those who aren't aware.

Embracing knowledge of the TRUTH is a priceless gift
For you will be hired &
- won't be fired -
because other spirits you will up-lift.

Dedicated to The Missionaries

~Heather Aguilar
© November 6, 2009

4

GUIDE US TO GLIDE

We always go by what you say.
We trust you will show us the way

To master the exams you give to us
So we can PASS the class
Without a huge fuss!

Dedicated to Professors

~Heather Aguilar
© December 5th, 2020

Uplifting Life

I cannot conduct life
Without any support.
With you as my guide,
I have not been cut short.

Your talent to see what another may need
Is a blessing to everyone whose mind you have freed.
From this world you have taken the burdens and strife
Of deciphering how to deal with stress in this life.

For it is you who have shown me the way to the path
To follow after enduring cerebral aftermath.
You are truly blessed and should always be
For your talents are truly Heavenly.

Dedicated to Beverly Kmiecik

~Heather Aguilar
© June 03, 2004

Eyes Mesmerized

There's a chance a gaze
may mesmerize
The eyes of another as they visualize

The gleam of sincerity
glowing facts within
Sharing knowledge that
chances glances
may not happen again

~Heather Aguilar
© December 5th, 2020

Fire-Glow Glasses

Your friendship I treasure
deep within my soul.
You are my soul-mate friend,
of course you know!

Don't ever belittle yourself from within
For your power is a
fire-shaped flower, dear friend

You can mold,
You can weld,
You can make this world glow.

Just look above this world,
And let your light show.

Dedicated to Kimberly

~Heather Aguilar
© July 11, 2005

DESIRE to ASPIRE to SLEEP with Smiles Soaring HIGHER

It's the annual season to
get caught up on the past –
Time seems to <u>fly</u> by <u>illegally</u> fast.

I'm focused on acquiring
complete control
Of my ridiculous
brain-managed sleep cycle.

~Heather Aguilar
© December 5th, 2020

FORGOT to REMEMBER

I don't always remember
- I don't-
If I did, I wouldn't forget!

~ *To*: Me, *From*: Me

Heather Aguilar
© December 18, 2009

REMEMBER I FORGET

Remember, I don't remember!
If I did, I wouldn't forget!

~ *To*: *Me*, *From*: *Me*

Heather Aguilar
© December 18, 2009

FOCUS ALIGNED ~ ALONG PATH DIVINE

Many people have looked at me
with an angular glance
After having been given my Life History
with my desire to enhance

Often times they see me 2be insane
Since I'm a single mom with only ½ a brain.

Well, of course I'm CrAziE! Wouldn't you be 2?
If you had lived the life that I've lived thru?!?

~Heather Aguilar
© December 5th, 2020

Chance to Glance

Honestly, I'm waiting to be with a man
with a strong & positive SOUL,

Whom I can stand beside, laughing during life
and in a friendly manner his hand hold.

For there are many trials everyone encounters
while traveling through this LIFE

When one trips then another may catch them,
helping one another to survive.

I haven't met a new man whose heart, soul,
and mind might match mine too.

Remembering the glimmer in your glance
my heart thought:
"It just <u>might</u> be <u>you</u>!"

~Heather Aguilar
© January 5, 2010

Life's Brush with Death

In 1970 a couple decided to adopt a newborn baby as their first child. An adoption agency informed them on August 13th, 1970 that a baby girl was born on August 9th, 1970 in Fort Worth, Texas and was available for adoption.

The couple made the trip from Monahan to Fort Worth, Texas the following weekend. My mother and father were delighted when they saw a bright eyed baby girl and named her "Paula Heather."

On a *summer day*, while driving back to Monahan, Texas, an incident occurred which was scary to the parents and proved to be my 1st event to escape death. The event was seen as: "Baby Heather's 1st **'Brush with LIFE & _DEATH_'**." On a *summer day*, the three members of the new family, my parents & I, were driving down a hill-shaped embankment it started to rain which turned the roadway into a slippery, dangerous, artery adjoining a busy four-lane highway.

The family car continued down the steep incline, and the father was unable to negotiate an abrupt turn to enter the highway's merge lane. The rain water carried my surprised parents, along with me (their new baby) when their car was sent to *slide* drive straight across the four highway lanes of busy traffic. Surprisingly, my parent's automobile had traversed the maze of cars and trucks while eluding all harm, without a *scratch!*

My parents were truly thankful they were able to safely drive thru the downpour and live life having been blessed to **not** have an accident on the freeway.

#2

PERSEVERENCE
Pulls
ENDURANCE

Be Kind to Your Mind -
Take Time to Align

If you put things where they SHOULD BE
when you get them
~ that is <u>GOOD</u>!

So you'll find 'em when you need 'em
'cause you made it
~So you <u>COULD</u>!

~Heather Aguilar
© January 17, 2012

UNCLEAN MEANS ~ "MEAN"

Be kind to yourself, tidy up your things
you have accidently dropped.

A little does **ALOT** when you always
clean-up **ALL** of your little spots!

Display what you mean
By keeping your place clean!

Analyze what "MEAN" means,
and know in some ways
some things are "unclean"

So, *who* is it "mean" *to?*
You will <u>see</u> unclean things become
"MEAN" to <u>YOU</u>!!!

Dedicated to YOU,

~Heather Aguilar
© December 6th, 2020

CHEAT COMPLETE DEFEAT

If someone else often finishes
what **you** should do
you will <u>never</u> learn to correctly
live LIFE thru - for <u>YOU</u>!

Just CHEAT DEFEAT –
with your LIFE kept <u>NEAT</u>!
By doing so, you'll **WIN** more for you!
Your LIFE won't have any
negative issues!

~Heather Aguilar
© December 6th, 2020

CARD was SET to Reduce DEBT

Often removing
little bits of debt
Reduces the charges on the card
you used to earn credit

When your debt will lower
frequently to flow
Your family's happy smiles will
be viewed with a glow

~Heather Aguilar
© December 6th, 2020

"Hi!" Scores

"At least I'm "**A**"~nnoying ~

<u>**NOT**</u> "**D**"~nnoying!"

~Heather Aguilar
© April 1st, 2011

My Forever Spouse

How long does one search for
the spouse of their dreams?

LIFE's weeks, months & years last
"forever", it seems.

If one has known *true love* once-
before in their LIFE,

Will another search be an endless
search to survive?

While smiling at weddings,
my eye wrinkles do show.

My wrinkles create in my
heart more sorrow

Since my loneliness can't be seen, no one
will know how my sorrow does flow

~Heather Aguilar
© December 6th, 2020

Clean Dreams Fly Fast When Friendships Last

Now, if I chose MY OWN dream designs,
We'd be flying to an island in MY Concord Jet just fine!
Of course we'd have our friends flying with us too,
And the ocean waves below would be
swirling gorgeous blue.
The gourmet picnic lunch, packed in the ice chest,
Our shoes are off, our shades are on
- we look our stunning best!
With you I shared my dream information so
you may be prepared
If a negative event occurs, then you will know
how to set your LIFE fair.
My dreams design different times when
daily thoughts are flowing in my mind.
Since I care, I correctly find righteous ways for other's
frowns to smoothly unwind
Wishing you smiles thru, while you live to
uplift your esteem
I'll be your friend until the end and
THAT is MY TRUE ETERNAL DREAM!

~Heather Aguilar
© December 16th, 2020

UP or DOWN?
SMILE or FROWN?

YOU do have the right
to choose **YOUR** way to earn LIGHT.

You can choose to lose & end up in a FIGHT,
OR You can Choose the Right &
display that you are bright!

Please make sure you're honest while living
your FINAL PATH thru LIFE.
Do you want to be happy **OR**
live thru LIFE frowning with strife?

Your voice is your choice &
your actions are your choice too.

Please search your memories within yourself, so
YOU can see a **TRUE YOU!**

I am just here to share with others what
I **KNOW** to be **TRUE,**

Since I TRULY care,
I want what is BEST **4 YOU!**

~Heather Aguilar
© March 31st, 2011

My Friend 'RIBBIT'

I picked up a frog in the grass on my way to the car after Sunday School. I was about to learn a lesson about **frogs**. I captured the frog with my bare hands, named it 'Ribbit' and I had a pocket for him. I climbed into the Station Wagon with 'Ribbit' tucked into my pocket and sat in the second seat behind my parents with my sister and three brothers.

When we came into our neighborhood, my father allowed me to crawl into the back of the Station Wagon so I could roll down the window and allow 'Ribbit' to breathe fresh air. I held 'Ribbit' in the palms of my hands while I kneeled and leaned my arms on the open back window sill of the vehicle. 'Ribbit' was truly enjoying the air flowing over his smiling face. I noticed how muscular his hind legs were when he flexed them and suddenly, without any warning, *LEAPED* like a dare-devil out of the palms of my hands, *LAUNCHING* himself towards the pavement below. My jaw dropped open in utter dismay and I screamed to my dad, **"STOP!!! *RIBBIT LEAPED OUT*!!!"**

So my dad shifted into reverse, glided a ways back, and allowed me to hop out of the car to find 'Ribbit'. My mom and I searched in front, behind, beneath and around the Station Wagon, yet could <u>NOT</u> find 'Ribbit' ANYWHERE!

My mind raced to think about what could have *possibly* happened to my new friend, 'Ribbit'! I called my mom over to a large storm drain on the edge of the curb and explained to her that 'Ribbit' may have decided during the adventure of the ride to search for his family in the sewers below. Maybe too much air had made him dizzy and homesick. I didn't know what could have made him feel he should leap out, but something <u>must</u> have sparked 'Ribbit's' spirit to escape the ever-loving palms of my hands that had cuddled him.

Truly disappointed, with my head down and my lower lip puffed out, I plopped back into the Station Wagon to ride down the street to our Home. When we arrived, I slid out of the back of the automobile and closed the Station Wagon's door. Much to my dismay, I saw 'Ribbit' was plastered **FLAT** on the back tire in front of me. Oh, my GOODNESS, *I couldn't believe my eyes!!! Poor 'Ribbit'!!!*

My dad had given my buddy, 'Ribbit', a ONE-WAY TICKET to Heaven!!! I'm sorry to say, I had to tell myself that 'Ribbit' wouldn't and *COULDN'T* be hopping back MY WAY!!!

#3

DISTINCTIVE ASSOCIATIONS

Inspired to Soar Higher

"Acquire the Desire
to encourage Others
with Desire to Inquire
So SOAL's Scores
Will Soar Higher"

~Heather Aguilar
© December 8th, 2020

Share what's TRUE Fair so More SOULs Will be Aware

The reason I've been allowed
to continue to survive
Is to share what's TRUE with others
So they'll know to Choose the
Right while they are alive!

Life experiences share how SOULs
can receive blessings from on *High*
When one repents & is faithful, a GIFT
of POWER is earned to *FLY!*

~Heather Aguilar
© December 17th, 2020

ABSORB within PURPOSE Not SIN

Everyone needs to take the time
To relax their ♥& open their MIND
In order to absorb the VALUE of their "self"
And NOT absorb the WORLD with
Their values on a shelf.

Just analyze the meaning of
Your actions here on EARTH
Then YOU'LL more fully understand
The PURPOSE of YOUR BIRTH

~Heather Aguilar
© January 2, 2010

CTR

~ Choose The Right ~

Living LIFE thru while
focusing to NOT ever sin
is a *wise* way to LIVE
for _heavenly blessings_ to be
scheduled for you to *WIN!*

Choosing the Right
while focused to correctly
live LIFE through
finds REAL SUCCESS and earns
true eternal happiness too!

~Heather Aguilar
© September 29, 2020

Master Faster

Having been given TASKs to
work on in living LIFE
Recognize how completing them
flushes away STRIFE

With less to do
happiness flows thru!

When earnings are acquired
Smiles occur to earn more
so additional TASKs are desired

Dedicated to Riley & Tavienne

~Heather Aguilar
© December 22, 2020

Giggle Forever!

True friendships are priceless
So, recognize they are
a rare commodity.

Almost everyone understands each of their friends with
true lucidity.

Oh, smile, laugh and
giggle again!

For you will know in the end
You'll acquire your
"Forever Friend!"

~Heather Aguilar
© May 25, 2004

U R the Author of FAR

Step out & take a look -
Do <u>YOU</u> like your life's book?
<u>You're</u> the one with the pen!
So, if not, change the end!
Envision your decision:
<u>YOU</u> decide WHO YOU are!
*Simply Choose the **RIGHT***
*& **YOU** <u>WILL</u> comfortably*
*Go **F-A-R!***

~Heather Aguilar
© April 1, 2011

His Presents

One day when I was little
A leather braid I made
And wove it correctly together
So the leather would not be frayed

Then gently I set my art piece aside

It had been created with "expertise"
& pure pride.

"Why?" you ask. "Why do I have
rice heat packs when I sleep?"
They comfort me, easing memories,
soothing the pains I weep!

When my eyelids close,
gently I smoothly doze,
gliding into time surreal ~
My mind is at peace,
my heart is at ease, and His arm,
SO WARM, I do feel!

~Heather Aguilar
© January 8, 2006

SWEPT OUT TO SEA

1975 Galveston, TX

When I was 5 years old, my family drove to Galveston for a day on the beach. On a beautiful day it became overcast with clouds, and the beach was almost abandoned.

I had recently been given a gift from my parents to have my ears pierced. When I was approaching to enter the ocean in Galveston, my Mother told me, "Don't get your ears wet, because we *don't* want your ears to be infected from the recent piercing." So I focused to play on a sand-bar with a pail and hand-shovel, in waist-line shallow water.

I followed the men who were taking out the net to catch fish. The *waves* rose, the *tide* became active, with *currents*, the outgoing *tide* became *TOO* much and my feet slipped off the sand bar into *suddenly deeper water*. The *currents* were *too* STRONG and *so much seawater* carried me out to *sea* when I was 5.

I was swept further and further out into the ocean, seeing the land and the beach appeared smaller and smaller. I realized that my mother, who I viewed as about half an inch high on the horizon, she was running back and forth on the beach looking for me, yet frantic, not being able to find me.

The wind blew, the tide was pulling me further out to sea, and I could not see how anyone was going to help me, or rescue me. I also knew that I could not get my ears wet, so I prayed to Heavenly Father; "Heavenly Father, nobody can see me so no one will save me. Please fix my wet ears after I swim because they need to be dry. Forgive me & help me. Amen."

Then, I took a *deep* breath, put my head in the water, and started to kick and swim towards the shore. I was determined, worked hard, and continued to stroke, going back to shore. I had prayed to God to help me. So, Heavenly Father's guidance helped me to swim in the right direction when I had lifted up my head twice to follow His directions. After I had put my head under the 2nd time and continued to swim to shore, I was certain that I would not need to look up often and I did not stop stroking until I got to the sand-bars. I had only looked up twice, to see I was swimming in the right direction that God had helped me know.

When I arrived in shallow waters I came crawling out of the water on my knees onto the beach and threw up a *LOT* of water right next to where my mother was standing. I kept vomiting, and vomiting, about a gallon of sea water. I knew that I only pulled my head out of the water two times.

It was a *heaven ~sent* MIRACLE for me to be able to swim ashore to be able to *live*.

#4

GUIDANCE
from ABOVE

Catch the Right Flight

I'd love for you to catch with
me my after LIFE's
heavenly flight!

You can pay the ticket price
to SOAR high when you
Choose The Right.

Dedicated to Smiley Riley

~Heather Aguilar
© March 31st, 2011

Right Fright Flight

Where am I going? What flight did I catch? I was blinded
when we boarded, ~ and my Tickets: <u>THEY DON'T MATCH!</u>

An adventure of this sort must've already been discussed!
I can't declare to know to "where," or even make a fuss.

When I've been launched into the air, with only half (½) a
brain, "No memory of discussion" would signal:"<u>1/2 INSANE!</u>"

So, head resting to the side, I'll gaze thru the thick glass,
Scanning depots up ahead and not a question will I ask.

~Heather Aguilar
© May 18, 2010

Often ONEs Rise to Reign Games Wise

In TRUE essence Education is a game against Oneself

So it's important not to leave One's BOOKs
upon the BOOK shelf!

Absorbing knowledge accumulates One's tokens
for Life's game

Allowing One to wisely design how to make their
moves, their knowledge is what their
BRAIN has gained!

How winning One's OWN games results in them being
able to obtain their own personal reign!

While people's moves are being watched by others in
Life's game, others will see

How BOTH sides WIN in the end &
One's existence
is in GLEE!

~Heather Aguilar
© August 28, 2011

THE FORCE TO SOAR

Given strength, endurance, torture and chains,
Few can fathom intense and infinite pains.
Pray tell the force you specifically chose to obtain
is a special force required for others to gain.

We know you are committed, or that you plan to be,
To commit oneself to torture,
You must surely be crazy!
Our family's pride oh so does swell
For you will serve our country well.

Through the years you've scaled life's dangerous fears,
Alas, you had no time for tears
Specifically analyze every single line more
Whenever determined to receive
smiles that soar*

Dedicated to Seldon Jack

~Heather Aguilar
© May 21, 2004

44

❤ PLACID SERENITY ❤

Placid serenity envelopes the souls
Of ALL who've had the privilege of
<u>your</u> hand to hold.

*For angels on high selected **you** for us*
To show us the way to return to Jesus

May peace be in your heart and your
smile always bright,

For we know your son, our brother and
Friend has walked toward the light

And we will be happy with him again.
Together forever, we'll be in heaven.

We are a Happy Family!
Sealed in the TEMPLE to be
"Together Eternally!"

Dedicated to My Heaven-sent Parents,
Mike & Maeveen Jack,
& My Forever Brother, Jeret Jack

~Heather Aguilar
© September 12th, 2002

45

Healthcare to Share

As life travels through time,
Trials fall into place,
Granting space to receive blessings
from those serving with grace.

To know in one's heart
they're here to help you,
Experiencing their dedication
and loyalty true,

Often times yields a relation divine
for as a patient, you're set,
and will be through time.

What an honor it is to receive
direct guidance fair
to be under your care,
For blessings of service
from angels is rare.

Dedicated to Dr. Sweeney, D.P.M. & Staff

~Heather Aguilar
© March 20th, 2006

Maintain to Gain

I need to make a living,
but I need to live to make it through.
Did I really ask for all these tasks
set up for me to do?

Well, I can't complain ~ there are funds to gain.
So, where's the next task at?
I had all the jobs listed,
set-up neatly ~ not twisted.
Now, where is the brand-new map?

Ah! Box #3 ~ All is in order I see!
I'll get things done,
life will be just fun!
So it's the perfect plan for me! (Hee, hee!)

Dedicated to Don Huot

~Heather Aguilar
© March 3, 2011

Soul's Goal within Raise Praise with Grins

When the process of your
goal was set into place,
YOUR divine dedication
was installed for your race.

Then you aligned your mind along
your long path & pressed GO!
All who saw you said, "FLY SLY FASTER
to master your GOAL!"

There was NO OTHER who could
have completed YOUR GOAL,
Since your secrets designed,
were tucked sublime within
your sacred SOUL!

Dedicated to Don Huot

~Heather Aguilar
© August 5, 2012

A Touch of Comprehension
Offered a New Dimension

Thank-you for offering me
the chance to "re-finance"
The option appeared clear
as one "to-go" at a glance.

For the terms and conditions set up
a deduction in the final cost,
However records of actions to complete
the procedure will have to be lost.

Adjustments cannot occur
at this time
Adjustments of procedures are
focused on to be set inline.

Your service was truly honest,
knowledgeable & pure
I wish you all the best in your life
and thru existence for sure!

Dedicated to Kayde

~Heather Aguilar
© May 10th, 2012

FLEET of FOOT Athletics: ...and SOCCER!

Speed is a requirement of the Right Wing position, which I played in Soccer. I was blessed with natural speed, so I played Right Wing. As an *offensive striker*, I passed, centered, and dribbled the ball with, and to my team-mates.

In addition to trying to steal the ball on defense, my speed and agility were most notable in leading the ball towards our team's goal blocked by the defenders. Many gifted athletes retain memories of specific instances of their athletic events. Most notable to my memory are the *cross-field passes* to teammates enabling them to score. Recognizing the opportunities to sleekly *slide-pass* when running *full speed* towards a goal, while Defenders are in the way, involves extraordinary maintenance of ball-control. Imagine leading a Team Mate cross-field with an OFF-Balance *instep kick* to launch-pass the ball to the far side, immediately in front of the goal at net-post height. This allows a match-paired teammate to complete the planned execution of a practiced play, by *launching himself*, while running *full speed*, to chest-rebound, jump-swing kick, or impact the ball with a forceful header into the *NET* for a SCORE!

This requires perfect execution of the ingenious and highly-practiced forms of intelligently shrewd competitive plays. From the individuals, it displays a remarkable level of sportsmanship, unselfish teamwork, as well as a clever aptitude, and reciprocal cooperation.

I also enjoyed playing drenched to the skin in the Malaysian monsoon rains, on a *muddy field*, and being able to slide-kick a ball for an astounding score! Reminiscing and recollecting awesome *steals*, *saves*, *high jumps* with *raised knees* are indicators of being significantly proficient in "talent and heart."

"And remember, they *always* made *me* run *LAST!!*"

#5

Children of
ALL Ages

When ALL is Done,
Life is Fun!

When _your_ actions
are made totally _complete_,

They can't conquer you
with their future _defeat_!

~Heather Aguilar
© December 8, 2009
2009

CHEAT DEFEAT WHEN YOU COMPLETE

You can present
the fact you are wise.
Also avoid scholastic demise

When **you** complete <u>ALL</u> tasks assigned
furning them in at <u>the right time</u>!

<u>You</u> will be happier
when each task is DONE,

For it relieves a burden
granting time to have **more fun**!

~Heather Aguilar
© March 20, 2010

Wings Prevail to Lift Those Who Ail

Friends have served as
"Angels" in our life,
They helped us endure
Our overwhelming strife,

We're blessed to
have them as our friends,
And we'll be beside _**them**_
until the end!

~Heather Aguilar
© May 19, 2009

Friendships True
Helped Us Through

We appreciate the service
You've gifted our family
For with your kind support
We've acquired sweet memories.

You've shown to us a friendship
That we cannot leave behind
For your priceless smile
is there all the while
& you're often on
OUR minds!

~Heather Aguilar
© August 22, 2008

They Know
You'll Glow!

In LIFE it is a blessing to
have missionaries near
For they're Angels sharing
the church that's TRUE &
their gospel is clear.

While they are helping others
They're absolutely sincere
Because it's their style
To often "smile"

And their comfort inspires
others is SO dear!
The clock tick-tocks as
LIFE flows thru ~
and they serve others the
gospel that's TRUE.

~Heather Aguilar
© December 23rd, 2020

The PYRAMID's TREE
Is Where The HORSE
THREW ME

Growing up in Malaysia I (Heather) absorbed the talent to avidly play soccer and baseball with boys and girls my age. I had learned to jump horses English-Style when I was growing up from 8-15 years old. When I was 15 I was politely informed by a person who trained me that I had "become a strikingly attractive young lady with a beautiful *tan* and a swift prize-winning Martial Arts Kick to quiet interested strangers." I was trained with my father and 4 of my siblings by a private instructor at our home which was next to the jungle in Kuala Lumpur. I as well as my father and 3 of my 4 brothers, earned Black Belts in Tae-Kwon-Do.

In January, 1991, when I was 20, I was studying *French* in New Jersey, while living with mr parents. To pull together my plan to study in southern France during the Fall Semester of 1991, I worked 4 jobs during the summer to earn the required funds. Shortly after I departed to live in Montpellier, France my parents were relocated by Exxon to live in Cairo, Egypt.

After completing 3 months of living in Montpellier to improve speaking French, I spent time with my family in Egypt prior to attending college at The University of New Mexico in Albuquerque. One of the standard tourist delights in Egypt was to pay the cheap price of $3.00 to ride a horse or a camel and be guided across a section of the desert in front of the

3 Pyramids. My father's supervisor owned several horses. He did not often have enough time to travel to the edge of Cairo in order to exercise his stallions. He politely requested

for his son, Chris, who was also in town, and me to exercise the 4 horses. One afternoon in January, 1992, Christopher & I were picked up and driven in a limousine to the stables near the Pyramids.

I selected the White Arabian stallion and decided to ride *bareback* since I had been professionally trained English-style. Both Chris and I decided to venture behind the Pyramids where the tourists did not travel. I was on the stallion, bareback, when we ran the horses wide-open towards the back of the Pyramids and "stumbled upon" a large acreage of land that had a *deep* indentation. As soon as we approached the side of the embankment, we saw it was a "Dead Horse Pit" of Tourist Horses. My horse saw the horses stacked upon each other, DEAD from having *not* received enough food, nor water, and being mistreated in a way that is against all ideas of righteous care. Astonished by the sight of so many Dead Horses, the horse I was riding fearfully bolted BACK galloping towards the corral.

Clenching the startled Arabian Stallion with my thighs and clasping onto the mane, hanging onto the reins, I was hoping the galloping horse would *SLOW* down. I realized the horse was focused on entering the stables. The only stables located by the PYRAMIDs in Cairo straight in front of the stallion had a tree dividing the ENTRANCE and the EXIT. The *Gatekeeper* of the stables was standing directly in front of the ENTRANCE side on the right side of the TREE, waving his arms to assign me to reduce the momentum of the horse's solid galloping towards the ENTRANCE. The stallion was dead-set focused on galloping full-speed into the safety of the corral.

As I approached the right side of the tree, set as the ENTRANCE, I pulled harder on the reins to slow the horse down from galloping into the manager standing in FRONT of the entrance on the RIGHT. The horse shifted wildly to the LEFT, bolting into the EXIT side in order to avoid the gatekeeper and the One Tree set there in the *desert*. I was flung off the stallion, did ½ a summer-sault in the air and was hurled to roll high-speed into the tree. I hit the back of my head on the tree causing a serious open wound, which bled profusely.

I was taken to the "Al Salaam" Hospital - the "Hello/Good-bye" Hospital (with the same meaning as the Hawaiian word "Aloha.") To be treated, having my head stitched I had removed ALL jewelry, except my GOLD anklet clamped to my left ankle. The doctor informed me that the *laceration* would require 13 stitches. I politely requested to receive a Localized Anesthetic; NOT to be put under a General Anesthetic. After the doctor had the female nurse insert an IV into the vein of my left arm, the doctor firmly stated, "You will start to feel VERY sleepy now as so need be for surgery." Then he stepped aside to the back of the room to discuss insurance terms and restrictions with a representative from Esso, the company where my father works.

While I was feeling disheartened, knowing I *would fall asleep*, I noticed that the male Medical Assistant was "eyeballing" my 24 Carat Gold Ankle-Bracelet clamped around the base of my right ankle. He rapidly filled a syringe, half with AIR and half anesthetic, in an attempt to rapidly put me to sleep so *he* could steal my ankle-bracelet before the doctor returned from his discussion to complete the surgery. (The value of my ankle-bracelet would increase the Medical Assistant's family funds and could possibly help them acquire more food for 7-9 months!)

Right before he was going to insert the needle into my IV line, ready to press the tip, I noticed the syringe was 1/2 filled with AIR and I knew *I* would *DIE* if AIR was injected into my blood stream. As I was just about to fall asleep, I reached towards the syringe he was holding and yelled out, "No! You can't do that!" I caught a glimpse of the surgeon turning his head to glance towards me, and started running back towards me before I fell asleep and I could NOT quickly grab the syringe out of the Medical Assistant's hands.

When I was awakened, my Ankle-Bracelet was _gone_ and they claimed that I did NOT have it there. After that event my heart was set NOT to wear *GOLD* anymore since it appeared to be "unlucky" for me, yet the value of GOLD helped other people. I survived the blow to my head and the attempt by the Hospital Attendant to _end_ my LIFE as another Miracle of Survival from my Heavenly Father.

[A CAT-Scan was performed at the "Al-Salaam" Hospital. The copy of the Cat-Scan was saved, even though the Doctors and Radiologists mentioned there was a very small ghostly image. The "foggy image, as seen through a mist" was determined to have *"no medical significance"* - that is, termed as "_unremarkable_!"] The small ghostly image was the foggy beginning of my Brain Cancer.

#6

Lessons of
LIFE's Instructions

Way May Sway

Not too far into Monday
My thoughts held a
tendency to
sway *His* way!

Kindly signifying in
my mind that in
my LIFE *He* may stay

Since it is "**Memorial Day!**"

~Heather Aguilar
© May 30, 2011

Holding on to Memories

How pleasant it has been to have
your presence near.
Your friendship is a treasure;
it's priceless and so dear.

You've helped so many through
the good times and the bad
To see your family leave
will truly be so sad.

Yet, you must know that LIFE
always continues on.
Your future moves you out,
so from here you must be gone.

Your smiles and your laughter,
we will surely miss,
and how will one ever forget
your amazing creativeness?

Just always know that wherever
your family may go
Memories of your family in our
Memory will be stowed.

Take care, travel safely, and forever stay strong.
We hope to see you again, dear friends,
before it's been too long!

Dedicated to: The Holder Family

~Heather Aguilar & Family
© November 1, 2005

Abstract Fact

When he does **not** retain within
His mind the concept of abstract,

He cannot be the one for me ~
And **that is** a *TRUE FACT*

~Heather Aguilar
© March 28th, 2011

Lace Laugh's Love

Laughs lift Life like
Love smoothly lingers
While smiles glow with each
touch of Laughs' fingers
Time need be for them to
comprehend our views
So, take the time to laugh &
Understand Laughs too!

~Heather Aguilar
© July 21, 2010

Spirits Pure Endure
LIFE Sure

For each of us to achieve
our individual success
We're granted our trials
in life to address.

With a pure desire of
success to acquire
We will recognize the
"trial lessons" true
That will guide us to acquire
our pure success too!

So the value of our LIFE's
"trial lessons" now & here
Completed correctly
grants priceless
Eternal Success
SO Clear!

~Heather Aguilar
© April 24, 2011
Easter Sunday

SOUND GROUND

I *LOVE* the way
the thoughts in
OUR minds
often spin
rOund!

For *our* ♥hearts♥ may
gleam smiles
with *Our* SOULs
scheduled to *soar to*
Heaven's **ground!**

~Heather Aguilar

Your Guidance Will Go with the Armadillo

This is **not** a payment,
Nor is it a bribe.
It stands as a sure symbol
Of the service
YOU provide.

For even though I move slow
along with my hard shell,
You've devoted sincere efforts
to motivate ME well!

Through these severing years in life
In my life you have invested
Self-motivating values
Eloquently unexpected.

So please allow the Armadillo to
Symbolize how in Life's Path
You've succeeded
guiding to graduation
One with Cerebral Aftermath!

Dedicated to Beverly Kmieck

~Heather Aguilar
© July 28, 2010

Train Yourself ~
It's on the Shelf!

I just need that **ONE PIECE**!
That **ONE** important piece was
right *here* on Tuesday
My sister must've grabbed it,
so I'll call her today!
But *WAIT!* It *might* be buried
in the closet collection drawer.
I *know* that I will find it
when I **pour it on the floor!**

#%Bz$7#@*!

Now, *I* am the **MASTER** of
MY own space!
So *I'm* the detective on this special case!!!

"Let's go!" Oh no!
I'll just grab a *NEW* towel
when I *zoom* out on my way!
I know a sleek-smooth plan
to get out fast today!

Slide the corner, sprint the hall,
towel closet's just right there.
Yank closet door open ~
WHOA! ~ I have to stop & **STARE**.
These towels are used for fun
& so are the games.
They share the same closet so,
"FUN CLOSET," is the name.

I should have thought to look
WHERE the piece _should_ **BE**!
THE PIECE I'd been looking for
was **STARING** straight at _ME_!

"A-la-YIKES!!! I cannot even _SEE_ YOUR BEDROOM FLOOR!!!!
ALL MUST be clean before YOU step outside YOUR door!"

If I always put things _where_
I knew they should BE,
I would _always_ be able to find them
pretty quickly.
_SO_, if I always put things away
when I'm _DONE_
THEN, I'd have a lot more time
to have _A LOT more_ FUN!!

**Dedicated to: Those Who have Pledged
NOT to be Missing ONE Piece**

~Heather Aguilar
© June 28, 2010

Feeding Jungle Monkeys

In 1977 my father, who worked in the United States, was transferred to work in Kuala Lumpur, Malaysia. A year later, when I was 8 years old, my father drove my mom, my 3 brothers, my sister & I into the jungle. There is a lot of jungle in Malaysia, some growing creepily up close to homes. My dad liked adventures and we were never sure what animals we would come across in the jungle. Dad parked the car on the side of the road beneath some large trees. As soon as we hopped out of the car, we noticed the chattering of monkeys and saw them swaying in the trees. The monkeys seemed as curious to see us as we were to see them.

My dad had brought a loaf of store bought bread. He gave me a couple of slices to feed the monkeys and he also had some slices and he had me hold the bag with the remaining bread. It seemed like those monkeys noticed we had something for *them* and *more monkeys* showed up. They were so *noisy* with their chattering and it was difficult to watch ALL the monkeys since they swung and jumped from tree to tree.

When my father was walking a ways in front of me he held his hand up and a monkey grabbed the bread he was holding. Focusing to give another monkey some bread I held up a piece of bread in my hand, hoping a monkey would be curious enough to approach me and pinch it out of my hand. ALL of a sudden the remaining loaf of bread was strongly *YANKED OUT* of my left hand by a monkey that had snuck up behind me!

In shock I was a little scared when I turned around. Then I saw the monkey thief had scampered back up a tree as other monkeys swung to him and tore open the plastic bag and bread fell down from the tree.

Our family soon left, but I will always remember this event as one of the many adventures my parents took us, their children on! "Family" is so important and while living LIFE I focus to stay emotionally close to them!

#7

LOVE & FRIENDSHIP

Clean Family Team

A house of diSoRdEr and complete disarray
Is a home to a family of utter dismay.
For how can a family within there abide
When one cannot find their room to reside?

A house of ORDER's members
focus on standards from above.
Disorder often flushes away
happiness & love.
When everything has a place of its own,
NO extras or true trash,
NO problems are sown!

Everyone *must* do their part of the task
without the others *always* having to ask.
For when each member
does *their* own little part
it shows their *love*
from inside their *heart*.

Families can work together as a team
so their home can appear _and_ truly be clean!
How wonderful it will be
to abide always together
with a loving, clean family team,
Together Forever......

~ Heather Aguilar
© March 5, 2008

Just Complete to
Cheat Defeat

When _your_ actions
are made
TOTALLY
COMPLETE

_Living LIFE thru
Choosing the Right
schedules you to
cheat defeat!_

~Heather Aguilar
© December 30, 2020

Retain NEAT &
Cheat Defeat!

It *doesn't* take much
To add *your* special touch!

Honestly,
it really isn't THAT hard!
Just *always* set things in
their <u>own</u> place~
Then it will make searches *very* easy
and you will have
MORE space!

Order you'll maintain
if you **do** this every day.
More smiles you will gain
when YOU set your
home this way!

~Heather Aguilar
© October 28, 2009

RESTRAIN with REIN the HEAT of DEFEAT

Visualize with *YOUR* own eyes
a scene wherein **YOU** stand.
Extinguisher clasped with
YOUR own grasp
controlled by
your own
hand.

A *test,* a *task,* a *trial*
– NO mask –is a fire set forth to face!
A choice does arise for **you** to surmise:
At what speed should <u>you</u> set *your own pace?*

Should you move slow & allow the warm glow
to grow & burn out your path?
OR should you reign with extinguisher's reins
to defeat forthcoming aftermath?

Your decision's precision defines a clear
line as to how **your life** will proceed.
Expose enlightened cool length
with a firm & set strength to
ensure on <u>your</u> path
you'll succeed.

~Heather Aguilar
© August 18, 2010

A Clean Menu
Can Be Seen

To serve you
the clean menu
is why I'm still alive.

Several times
I have been granted
the chance to survive.

The white fettuccini sauce
featured in this menu

Was created
with a GLOW
to share with <u>YOU</u>
*what's **TRUE!***

~Heather Aguilar
© August 6, 2009

Reveal the Meal

The Gourmet Dish has been designed
all ingredients within are aligned.
But to appeal to each new client
an image need be defined.

Your superior sketch talent would show
just what this taste will say.
Each ingredient flings a separate
flavor that sings
You could capture just what to portray.

Now, the glow is at a pilot flame
for things to fall in place.
Would you consider drawing
in the menu with
your own personal grace?

~Heather Aguilar
© May 20, 2010

A Shot of Comprehension
Serves a New Dimension

Thank-you for giving me the gift to
__more__ fully understand
The functions of my brain and
__how__ it comprehends.

For since the terms and meanings often
held some similarity,
when I tried to reference them, they were
dim in my mind's memory.

Material couldn't be absorbed
within a short time
Yet, within 3-months my mind
will taste the words & set
memories to be aligned!

You've provided me with fuel
so that I can make it through!
Best of luck to you
and all your friends too!

Dedicated to Missionaries

~Heather Aguilar
© June 26, 2009

Dedication Due Ovation

Having been presented
with an overwhelming task,
I ventured to your office and
didn't even have to ask,
for you kindly offered me assistance
with insight from the start,
your dedication to resolve
The Task apparent you did impart.

Not only did you gently repaint
the picture for me to see,
You also sacrificed YOUR valuable time
to make ALL matters work for me.

There isn't a word in any
language that I know
To describe a person like yourself
with such an AWESOME glow!

I express to you my gratitude for ALL
the assistance that you have given me.
For even though I don't always recall,
your glow's forever etched in MY memory.

Dedicated to Jane

~Heather Aguilar
© May 21, 2009

ZOOM ZIMMERMAN!

For every course you teach,
YOU know each word.
But the pace you reach
for my brain's absurd!
I only hold half a brain
within my head to plan.
It's impossible for me
to completely understand
All the relationships you've
interwoven across
When I have within my mind
Short-Term Memory Loss.

Please forgive me for
dropping words before
finishing the rest.
I venture on to correctly set words
to pursue the quest.
The speed limit will
be legal - without
stumbling as I run.
My brain will smile
all the while and I'll
work to have more fun!

Dedicated to Prof. Zimmerman

~Heather Aguilar
© February 19, 2009

You Turn

Sometimes this world sparkles with gleam,
The treasures you "see" are NOT what they *seem*.
For before from Above
You descended
to Earth,
You passed through a veil,
leaving past knowledge at birth.

Then a blink and a snap and
back to NOW & HERE
Another long pause, life still appears SO *unclear*.

Trapped at the end of the street at a RED,
Tapping your fingers,
you peered at a light up ahead.
With turn signal ON, green arrow clicking RIGHT,
RED changes to GREEN &
you STARE at the light.

"I CAN'T remember which direction to GO!"
"I don't know, in fact, if I EVER did know!"
Your car inches forward, cars honking behind,
Passengers in back mutter statements spoken kind.

Ever SO slowly the tire rims spin.
Immediately, clouds darken and sky above dims.
Eyes flick to the lights ~ YELLOW,
then RED does appear.
More honking; more screaming...
"I should have gone ~NOT be here."
So, patiently you wait for the light to turn GREEN.
Nails clicking, click~clicking, forever it so seems.
Then, to GREEN it turns & rubber you ***BURN!***

Looking back? Why should you?
For your stomach to *churn*?

You hear cheers from behind,
for you **didn't** turn right!
But, you glance to the side
to where you SHOULD have gone,
to see a gorgeous neighborhood
with Heavenly beams thereupon.

Eyes wide, you jerk back &
SCREAM out in fright~
"It is dark, you can't <u>see</u> in the middle of the night!"

Don't worry! <u>YOU'RE</u> driving ~
this journey's <u>YOUR</u> choice.
Just remember to **ALWAYS** listen
to the Still Small Voice.

And now know and always remember
within your heart, that this GIFT is TRUE.
With The GIFT of The Holy Ghost having been sent
you'll receive guidance correctly through!

Dedicated Highway Accident Survivors

~Heather Aguilar
© July 27, 2005

"Hanging 10" on Route 666 at "The Four (4) Corners"

On October 18, 1992, I was 22 years old, and had been living in Albuquerque, New Mexico attending the University of New Mexico. I had decided to drive to Provo, Utah to visit extended family members. On the way back home I was driving along Route 666 near: "The Four Corners" area in South-East Colorado.

While enjoying the ride driving my new "Conquest," which was the Prototype for the Viper automobile, I saw a *young deer* standing in the *right lane*, directly in front of *me*, so I swerved to the *left*. Then, the *deer* suddenly jumped to the *left lane*; and my reaction to avoid having the *deer* come *flying in thru* my windshield was to quickly swerve hard to the <u>right</u>; I became *air-borne*, flew *off* the <u>edge of the road</u> and *slid* into a <u>ditch</u> to the *right*. I attempted to correct the direction by rapidly *yanking* the <u>steering wheel</u> to the *left*. However, I was already caught in the <u>ditch</u> and was actually flipped three and one-half roll-overs, which ended with **me upside-down** in the car at the bottom of a steep embankment.

I had my seat belt buckled, but both of my arms had been broken in two different locations each, and I could not control ANY movement in my arms. My arms were hanging when I was trying to move to unbuckle myself. As I attempted to fold my broken arms, they swung and hit me in the face as they flew from the steering wheel. I laughed at how ridiculous it was for me to NOT have a way to get **out** of my car. I was upside down, with blood running out of my ears and seeping from the top of my damaged skull. The blood was drizzling down my skull, onto my face, and coming out strongly.

I crossed my broken arms causing them to fall into my face again and prayed to **Heavenly Father** to help me get out of my car. Pleading, I said to **Heavenly Father**, "Help me Heavenly Father; I don't want to bleed to death in this automobile with my arms broken on a frozen night in the middle of nowhere, and all-alone, except for **Thee**."

Having flipped **3 ½ times**, the roof was dented in, causing me to be permanently damaged on the top rear of my *cranium*. I had suffered a ripped-open slash and penetrating indentation at the top central area of my skull.

After expressing I wished for Heavenly Father's support I flung my *left* arm against my *right* arm and then swung them towards the seatbelt in an attempt to unbuckle myself, but it was **NOT possible**. Apparently, the overwhelming pain from the sharp movement of four broken bones caused me to pass out and lose consciousness.

[At this time, I experienced an "other worldly event" of Epic Proportion: being mystifyingly removed from the Wreck during a "Near-Death Occurrence."

I witnessed being apart from my trapped body – while

I was inexplicably lifted, freed, and set aside from the wrecked automobile.]

ed. Note- *Many refer to this as: "a Miracle."*

The next moment I remember, I was walking on thorns while I was trudging barefoot up the embankment towards the road level. My *left* arm was hanging below my knees with my *right* arm, broken from the elbow down, dangling as well.

Two men in a pick-up truck pulled over when they saw me walking on the side of the freeway with both of my arms broken. One stayed with me while the other drove to the nearest home to use their phone. Since cell phones were not yet created, he was able to call 911 & have an ambulance pick me up. The gentleman who stayed with me looked around in bewilderment and was shocked at the condition of my car. He pondered the question of just how did I ever get out of my upside-down car, and make it up to the road level with BOTH of my arms broken! I said I had said my prayers and Heavenly Father had helped me be able to exit the upside down car.

I was taken to a hospital and an MRI was performed. The **surgeon** and **radiologist** observed nothing extraordinary in the primary trauma injury. However, due to a unique circumstantial coincidence, four (4) Physician's Medical Samples of Titanium Rods were available to be inserted through the core center of each of the fractured bones in my arms. Even though my **left arm** had been hanging below my knees, I was able to recover the use of my **left arm's fingers** and today there is only a slight numbness remaining in my **left arm** occasionally. Both of my **arms, left** and **right,** are rather cold because of the metal rods installed within the center of their bones.

When my mother was in the Hospital she displayed pictures she had received from the Police Officer. He said, "Since Heather had unbuckled herself she must have fallen down onto the inside of the ceiling of the car which was covered with shattered glass from all of the broken windows. If she released herself, she would have surely fallen and **badly** cut herself." My mother inspected my back, and there was not even a scratch!

Heavenly Father had sent someone to release me and get me out of the car without a scratch. I had been involved in a MIRACLE of Rescue from Bleeding to Death.

#8

SOUL's SUPPORT

Click Align Spines Divine

If you have a kink or odd
pressure in your spine,
The doctor that you need is
the one who re-aligns.

Not only has she focused on
mastering every task,
She is very much in tune with the
questions that you'll ask.

~Heather Aguilar
© December 12, 2008

Forgot Knot

It is rather hard to remember
when you do NOT know
what you forgot.

One's concept of Life
becomes lasso'd
since all thoughts have
been twirled in a knot.

~Heather Aguilar
© March 29th, 2011

Unwind My Kind Mind

I cannot <u>rEmeMbER</u>
NOT to forget!

It's a PLAN my mind has NOT yet MET!

I'm dedicated to acquire
inspiration for ME...
...to live LIFE thru
completely correctly!

~Heather Aguilar
© May 5th, 2012

SUBLIME TIME

I forget I can't always remember.
But I remember I often forget!
Then, what I've said is not in my head
So, I know for sure it's time for bed!

~Heather Aguilar
© June 6th, 2011

*** How would you feel if you awakened and realized you'd been living with a skewed view of existence, and an altered perception of your position in life? Hence, is the LIFE you have one you would NOT have chosen?***

La-tee-dah

I sit asunder and I wonder,
"***Why*** is it I'm at home alone?"

"*How* can it ***possibly*** be
that no one's here & "Good-bye!" they didn't tell me?"

Time was <u>whistling</u> by...
as I let out a sigh,
when I remembered the
Shunt flushing in my brain causes me
to forget information I received recently.

Now I KNOW I need to contact a member of my family
to acquire information to smile happily!

I called and asked my brother,
"Why did you leave me by myself at home?"
He said, "We left you to go shopping
and allow you to sleep quietly alone!"

"La-tee-dah Time" is when I have an empty mind.
Then my sincere & humble prayers earn for me
guidance to know "***<u>what to do</u>***"
which adds smiles as I LIVE LIFE correctly!

Dedicated to Everyone Who Reads It!

~Heather Aguilar
© April 15th, 2021

P.S. ~ This POEM is an ***example*** of times in my LIFE &
I cannot remember if this event actually occurred.
Please remember I will NOT *"lie"* unto you.

A Kindergartner's Dream

You've done so much for my little girl,
You've opened her eyes and
shown her the world.

Soon into the world you
will be setting her free.
What you've done for her
means so much to me.

Thank-you for your time,
your gracias care & true love;
You're everything in a teacher
A Kindergartner could ever dream of!

Dedicated to Ms. Lehman

~ Heather Aguilar
© May 13, 2004

Smile All the While

Best of luck to you in <u>all</u> that you need to do,
My wishes are sincere that YOU
do make it thru!
For given <u>any</u> trials you may face in life,
You may have what <u>you</u> need to
conquer ALL of your LIFE's strife!

Every TRIAL is a weight
as you cruise along,
this will actually assist
in making YOU more strong.
Once TRIALS have been tackled,
pushed below, <u>and</u> behind,
one then acquires the sweet gift entitled,
"Peace of Mind."

~Heather Aguilar
© June 26, 2009

"LIFE Lessons from Above" Inspire Souls on Earth to Correctly LIVE LIFE thru!

My Poetry Lessons, which have been Stimulation for me to write, are often a stream-of-consciousness turned to very specific words and poetic stanzas with meanings that unfold to me as I write what I "hear" verbatim.

Writing Poetry became a joy to engage in more than an Artistic Impression when I was 13-14 years old. I enjoyed using my Gift!

At age 15-16 a certain understanding that the Artistic Expressions "may have been prompted to show me links to Life Events that were unfolding."

At ages 18-20, because of wanting to help my Mom, Dad, or a Good Friend in some obscure way, "I was only occasionally being prompted to write on a subject with insights and encouragement for assisting others to see a Vision for Inspiration." That's how I felt while on a slow and evasive path attending to others Spiritual Needs.

Around age 21 to 22 I felt "Writer's Block," or just plain difficulty in Brain Function. I experienced a few traumatic episodes which affected the course of my Life. The 4 Corners of the United States & Cairo, Egypt both required some considerable rehabilitation and Life Change.

Trauma rehab defeated Spiritual progress during the time-frame of age 22-23, while struggling to recover from head injuries in Egypt in January of 1992. This was compounded by the multiple fractures of both my arms and further head injury which I suffered while enduring the Triple Roll-over and the consequences of the Near-Death experience on Route 666 on October 18th of 1992. A "Mental Stagnation" period at Age 24-25, 1994-1995, of Cerebral Lethargy followed my *physical rehab* from these tragic occurrences.

An Amazing Transformation and Major Alteration of My Spiritually-Directed Capabilities flowed from the Events immediately following my 27th Birthday in August of 1997. The resulting rejuvenation of my Poetic Prowess was evidenced by a resurgence of Creative Energy, and the evolution of being prompted to write <u>inspired words</u> and <u>phrases</u> at all times of the Day and Night.

The promptings increased in Clarity, and the Quality of the Inspired Verses and Messages gave me the knowledge and confidence that I was now equipped to both receive and transmit Heavenly Dispatch.

In My 2nd Book of Poetry: "Spirits Pure Surely Endure," the <u>evidence of the evolution of my dedication</u>, Steadfast Loyalty, Communication Expertise, and Gifted Heartfelt Faith transpires to exhibit the Power of Other-worldly Mediations. (Book # 2: "Spirits Pure Surely Endure" will be released including another Heavenly Intervention of considerable impact.)

My following book, Book #3: "Treasures of Divinity SOAR =SOALs=> to PURE Infinity" is a religiously-categorized volume.